HAL•LEONARD®
GUITAR
PLAY-ALONG

AUDIO
ACCESS
INCLUDED

PLAYBACK+
eed • Pitch • Balance • Loop

T0039796

To access audio visit:
www.halleonard.com/mylibrary

6905-3025-9287-3148

Cover photo: Retna Images

ISBN 978-1-4950-4592-9

HAL•LEONARD®

7777 W. BLUEMOUND RD. P.O. BOX 13819 MILWAUKEE, WI 53213

In Australia Contact:
Hal Leonard Australia Pty. Ltd.
4 Lentara Court
Cheltenham, Victoria, 3192 Australia
Email: ausadmin@halleonard.com.au

Visit Hal Leonard Online at
www.halleonard.com

CONTENTS

GUITAR NOTATION LEGEND

THE MUSICAL STAFF shows pitches and rhythms and is divided by bar lines into measures. Pitches are named after the first seven letters of the alphabet.

TABLATURE graphically represents the guitar fingerboard. Each horizontal line represents a string, and each number represents a fret.

4th string, 2nd fret   1st & 2nd strings open, played together   open D chord

HALF-STEP BEND: Strike the note and bend up 1/2 step.

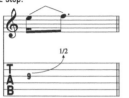

WHOLE-STEP BEND: Strike the note and bend up one step.

GRACE NOTE BEND: Strike the note and immediately bend up as indicated.

SLIGHT (MICROTONE) BEND: Strike the note and bend up 1/4 step.

BEND AND RELEASE: Strike the note and bend up as indicated, then release back to the original note. Only the first note is struck.

PRE-BEND: Bend the note as indicated, then strike it.

VIBRATO: The string is vibrated by rapidly bending and releasing the note with the fretting hand.

PALM MUTING: The note is partially muted by the pick hand lightly touching the string(s) just before the bridge.

HAMMER-ON: Strike the first (lower) note with one finger, then sound the higher note (on the same string) with another finger by fretting it without picking.

PULL-OFF: Place both fingers on the notes to be sounded. Strike the first note and without picking, pull the finger off to sound the second (lower) note.

LEGATO SLIDE: Strike the first note and then slide the same fret-hand finger up or down to the second note. The second note is not struck.

SHIFT SLIDE: Same as legato slide, except the second note is struck.

TRILL: Very rapidly alternate between the notes indicated by continuously hammering on and pulling off.

TAPPING: Hammer ("tap") the fret indicated with the pick-hand index or middle finger and pull off to the note fretted by the fret hand.

NATURAL HARMONIC: Strike the note while the fret-hand lightly touches the string directly over the fret indicated.

PINCH HARMONIC: The note is fretted normally and a harmonic is produced by adding the edge of the thumb or the tip of the index finger of the pick hand to the normal pick attack.

TREMOLO PICKING: The note is picked as rapidly and continuously as possible.

VIBRATO BAR DIVE AND RETURN: The pitch of the note or chord is dropped a specified number of steps (in rhythm), then returned to the original pitch.

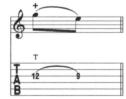

VIBRATO BAR SCOOP: Depress the bar just before striking the note, then quickly release the bar.

VIBRATO BAR DIP: Strike the note and then immediately drop a specified number of steps, then release back to the original pitch.

Additional Musical Definitions

(accent)   • Accentuate note (play it louder).

(staccato)   • Play the note short.

D.S. al Coda   • Go back to the sign (𝄋), then play until the measure marked "*To Coda*," then skip to the section labelled "**Coda**."

D.C. al Fine   • Go back to the beginning of the song and play until the measure marked "***Fine***" (end).

Fill   • Label used to identify a brief melodic figure which is to be inserted into the arrangement.

N.C.   • Harmony is implied.

• Repeat measures between signs.

• When a repeated section has different endings, play the first ending only the first time and the second ending only the second time.

5

Beyond the Realms of Death

Words and Music by Robert Halford and Les Binks

Intro

Moderately slow ♩ = 88

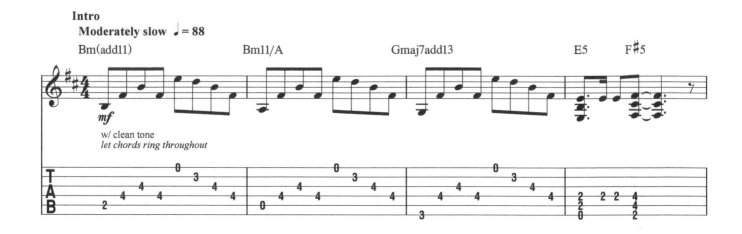

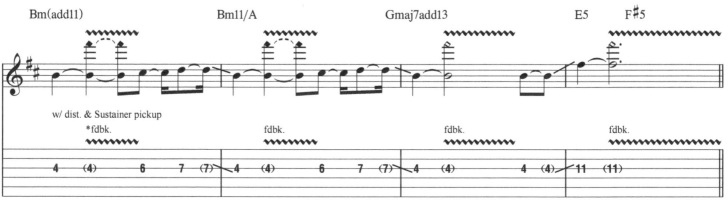

*"Feedback" overtones produced by Sustainer pickup in harmonic mode.

𝄋 Verse

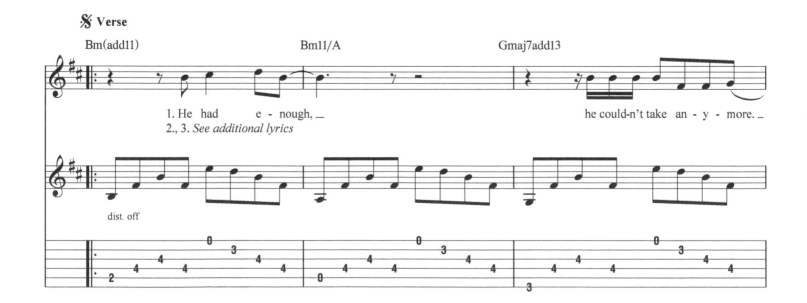

1. He had   e - nough, ___   he could-n't take an - y - more. ___

2., 3. *See additional lyrics*

dist. off

Chorus

hand.   Yeah!   I've left the world ___ be-hind. ___

I am safe here   in my mind. ___   I'm

free   to   speak   with   my own   kind.   This is

my   life, ___ this is my   life,   I'll de - cide, _ not   you. ___

*Swell in dist.

*w/ dist.

take for-ev-er, and ev-er, and ev-er, and ev-er, but I'll still win. _

Guitar Solo

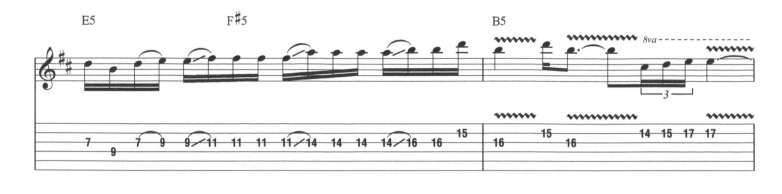

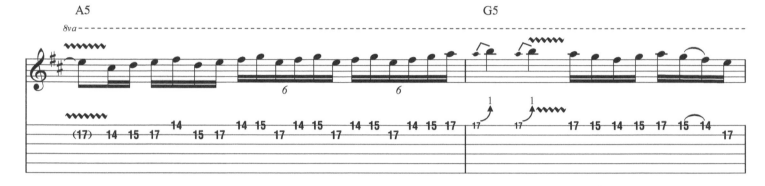

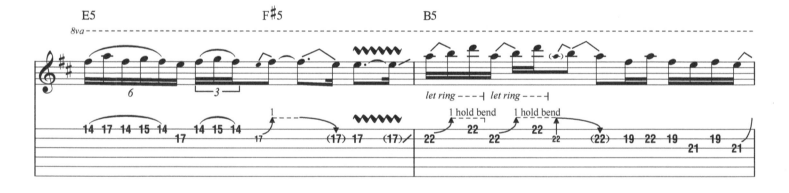

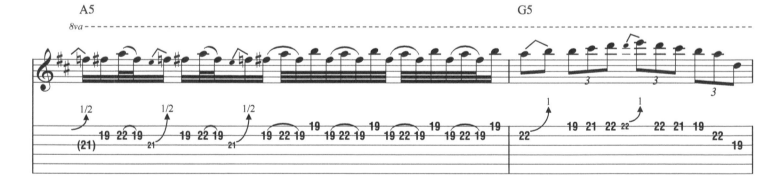

D.S. al Coda

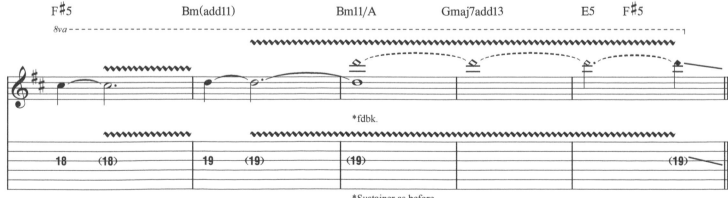

*Sustainer as before.

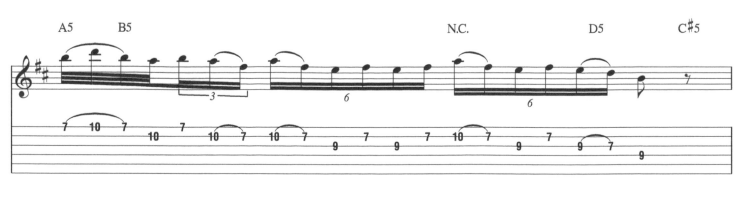

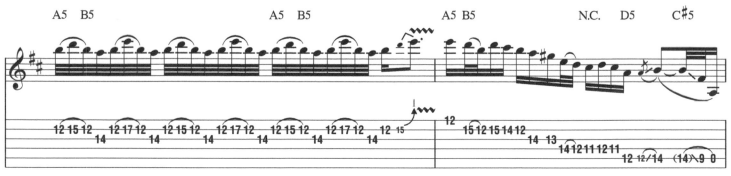

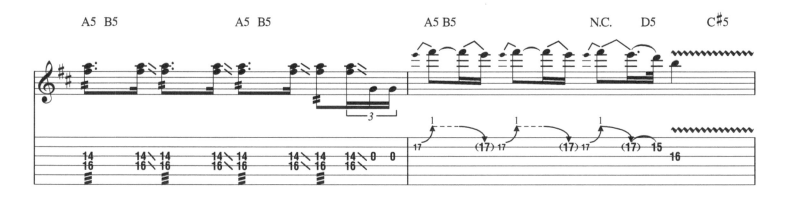

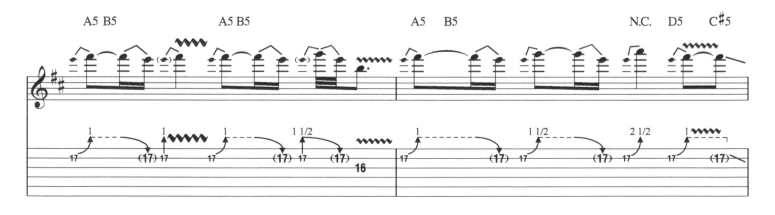

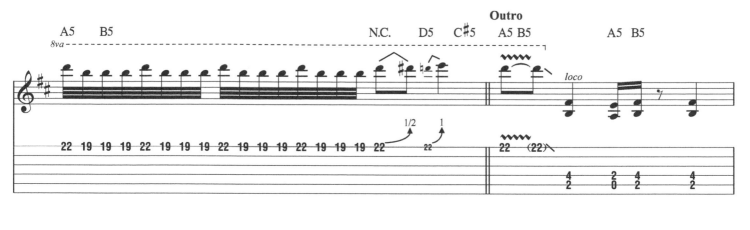

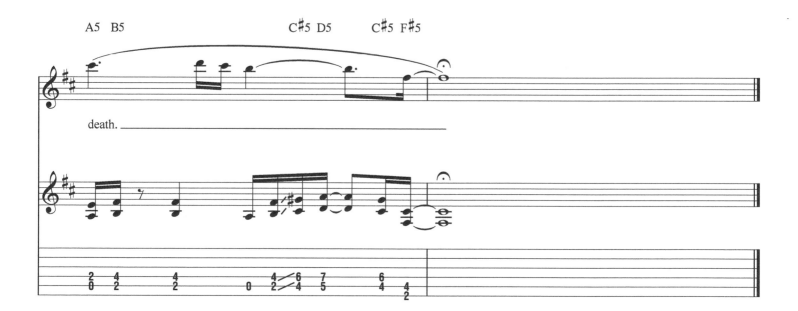

Additional Lyrics

2. Withdrawn, he'd sit there, stare blank into space.
No sign of life would flicker on his face.
Until one day he smiled, it seemed as though with pride.
The wind kissed him goodbye - and then he died.

3. How many like him are there still,
But to us all, seem to have lost the will?
They lie in thousands, plagued and lost.
Is nothing worth this bitter cost?

Breaking the Law

Words and Music by Glenn Raymond Tipton, Robert Halford and Kenneth Downing

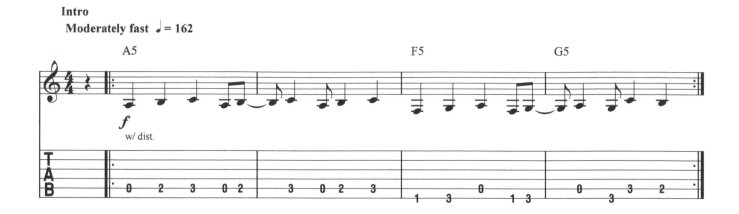

Delivering the Goods

Words and Music by Glenn Raymond Tipton, Robert Halford and Kenneth Downing

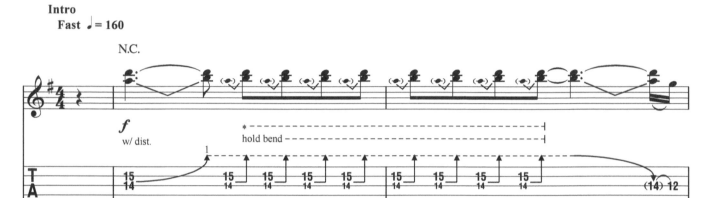

*Re-articulate w/ toggle switch

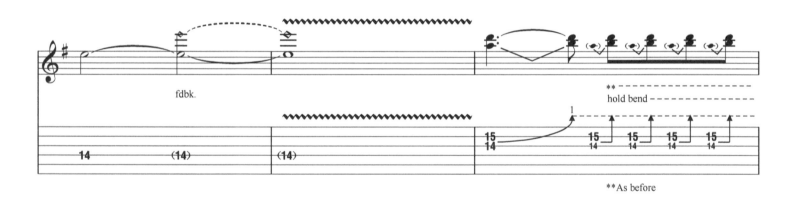

**As before

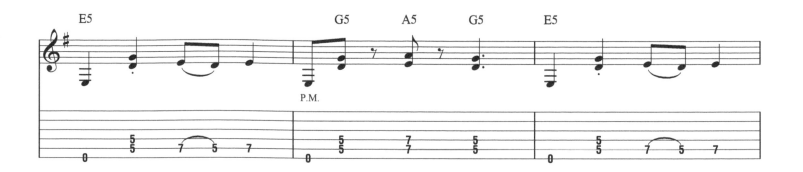

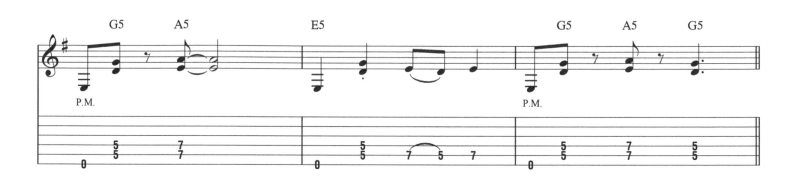

% Verse

1. Feel - in' ___ like ___ we're, we're read - y to kick to - night. ___
2., 3. *See additional lyrics*

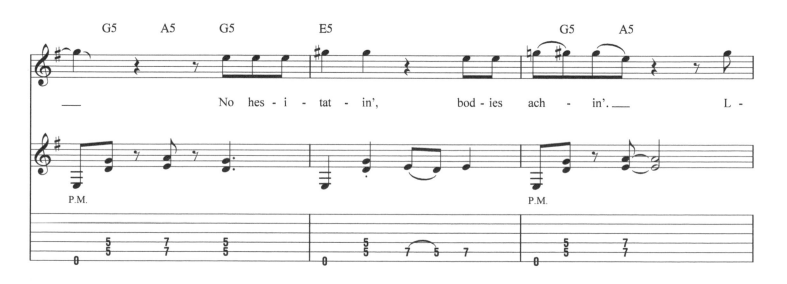

___ No hes - i - tat - in', bod - ies ach - in'. ___ L -

Guitar Solo

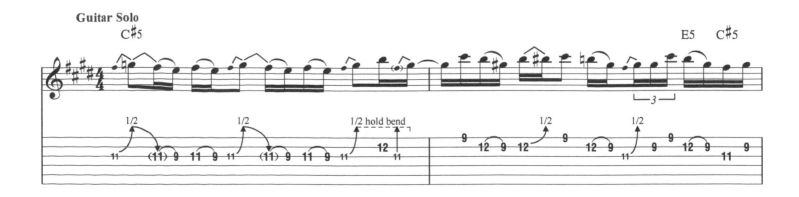

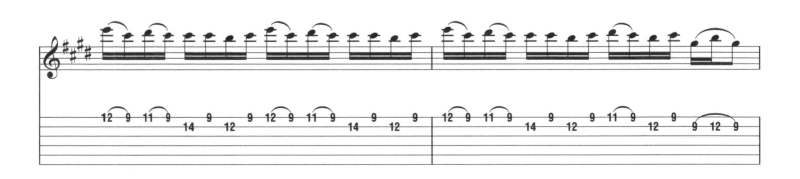

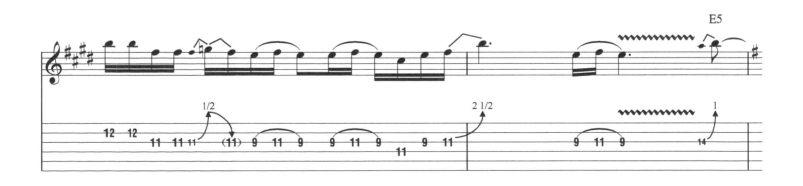

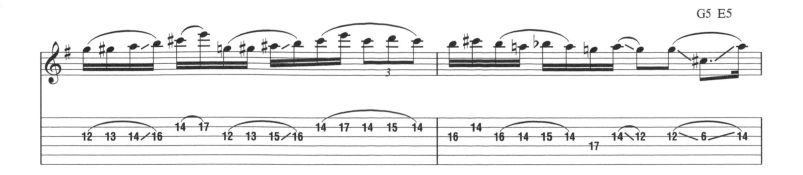

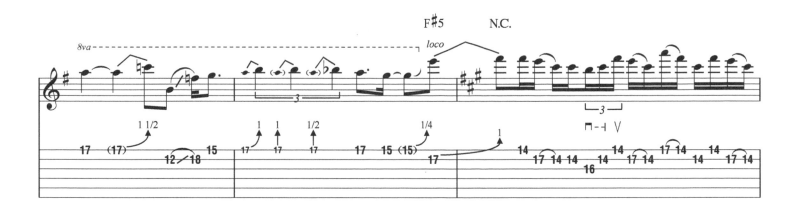

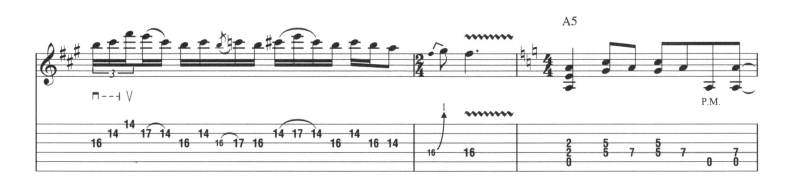

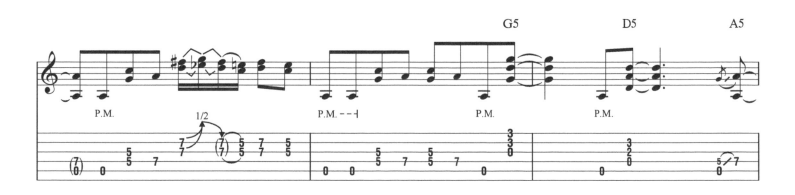

Bridge

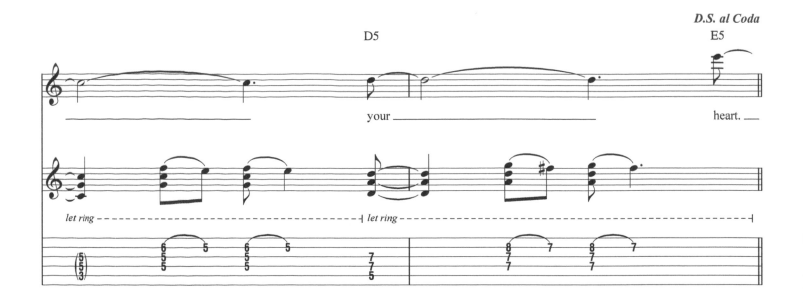

Coda

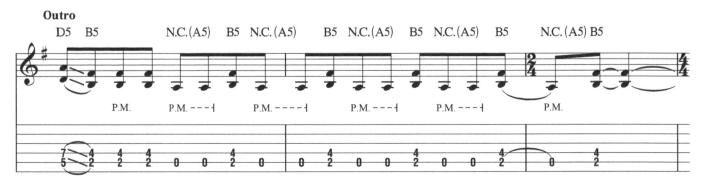

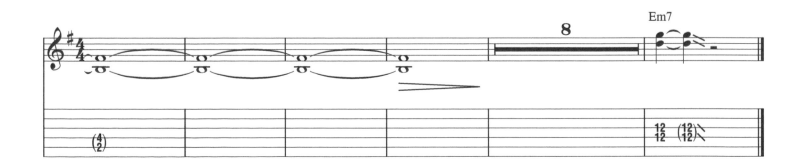

Additional Lyrics

2. Shakedown, rock 'em boys. Crack that whip strap mean.
   Pulse rate, airwaves. Battle lies in every place we've been.
   Stealing your hearts all across the land.
   Hot blood, doing good. We're going to load you with our brand.

3. Faster, higher, till it seems that we're gonna break.
   Oh, shootin' further. Giving more than you're ever gonna take.
   Leaving your heads crushed out on the floor.
   Begging for mercy. Be careful or we'll do it some more.

Electric Eye

Words and Music by Glenn Raymond Tipton, Robert Halford and Kenneth Downing

Verse

1. Up here in space
2. *See additional lyrics*

I'm look-ing down on you.

My la-sers trace ev-'ry-thing you do.

You think you've pri-vate lives, think noth-ing of the kind.

Pre-Chorus

33

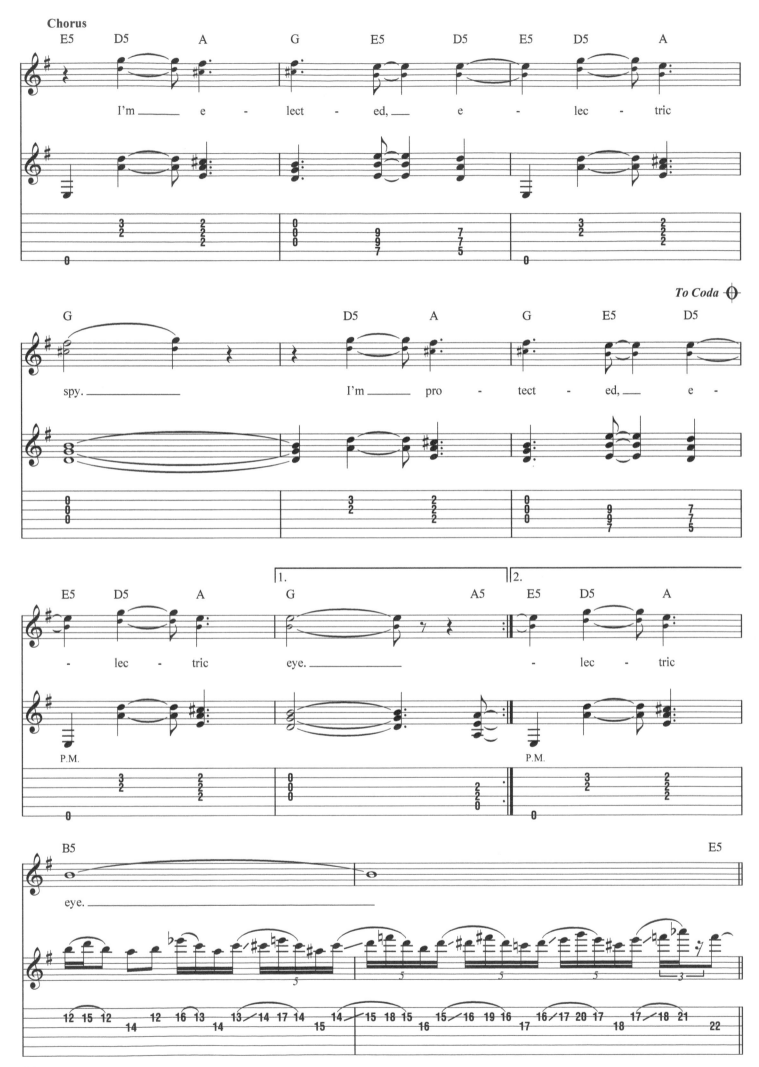

Guitar Solo

Interlude

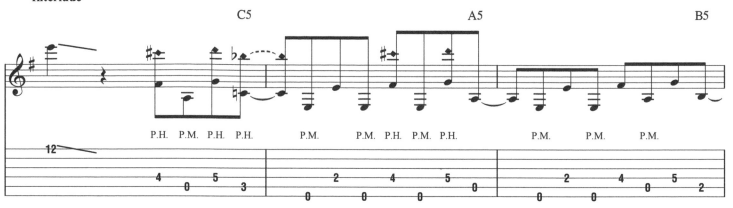

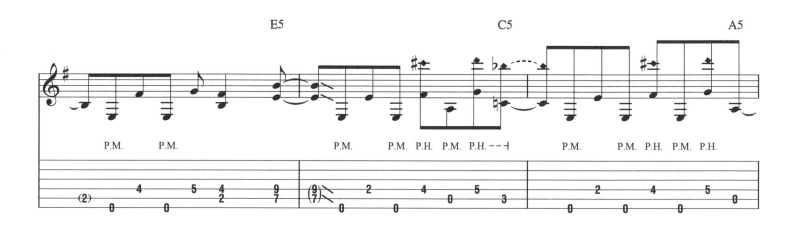

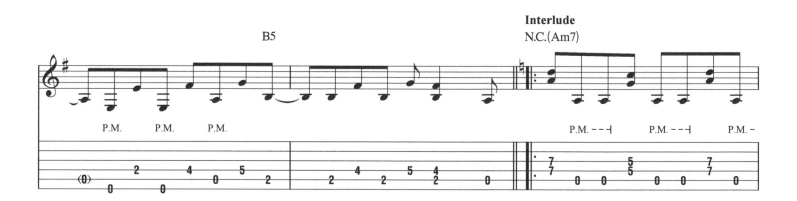

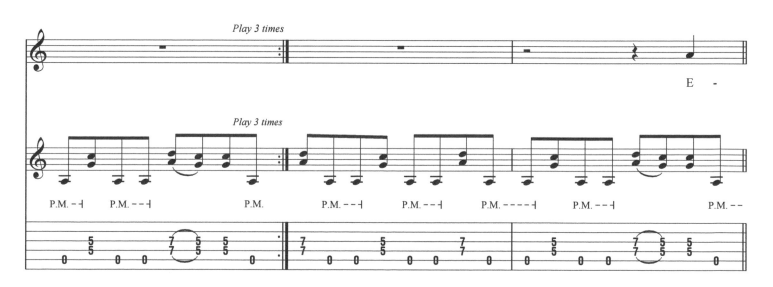

Bridge

Coda

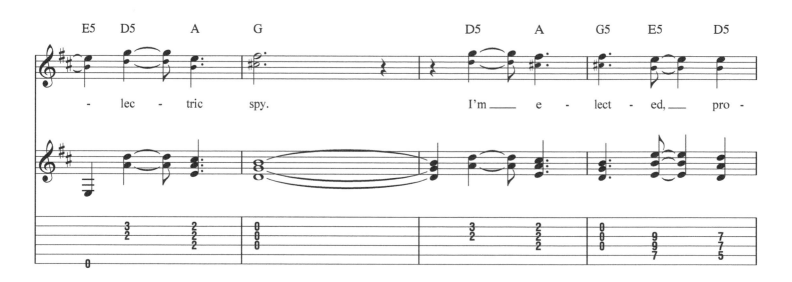

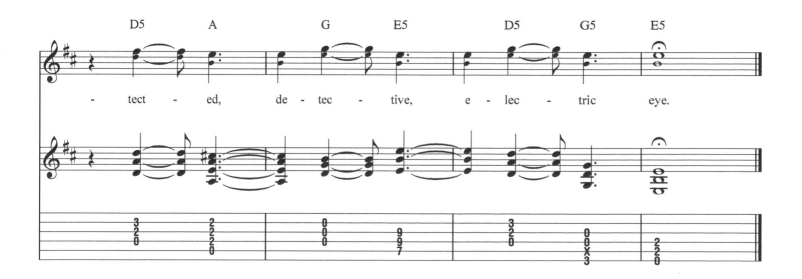

Additional Lyrics

2. Always in focus, can you feel my stare?
   I zoom into you, but you don't know I'm there.
   I take a pride in probing all your secret moves.
   My tearless retina takes pictures that can prove.

Heading Out to the Highway

Words and Music by Glenn Raymond Tipton, Robert Halford and Kenneth Downing

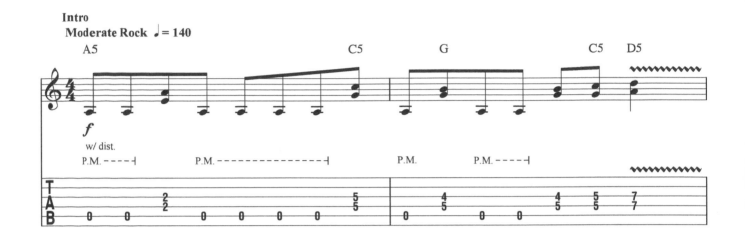

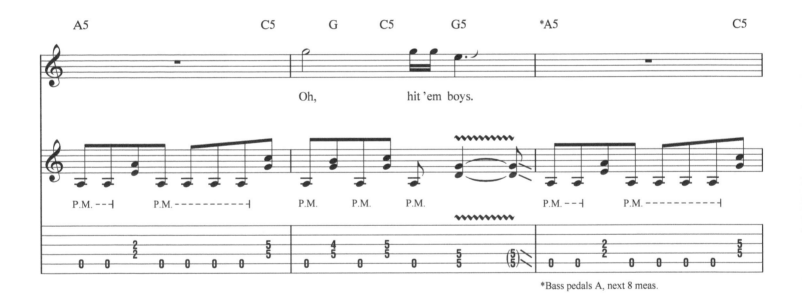

*Bass pedals A, next 8 meas.

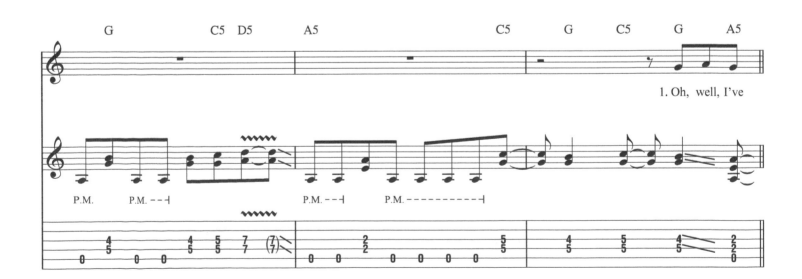

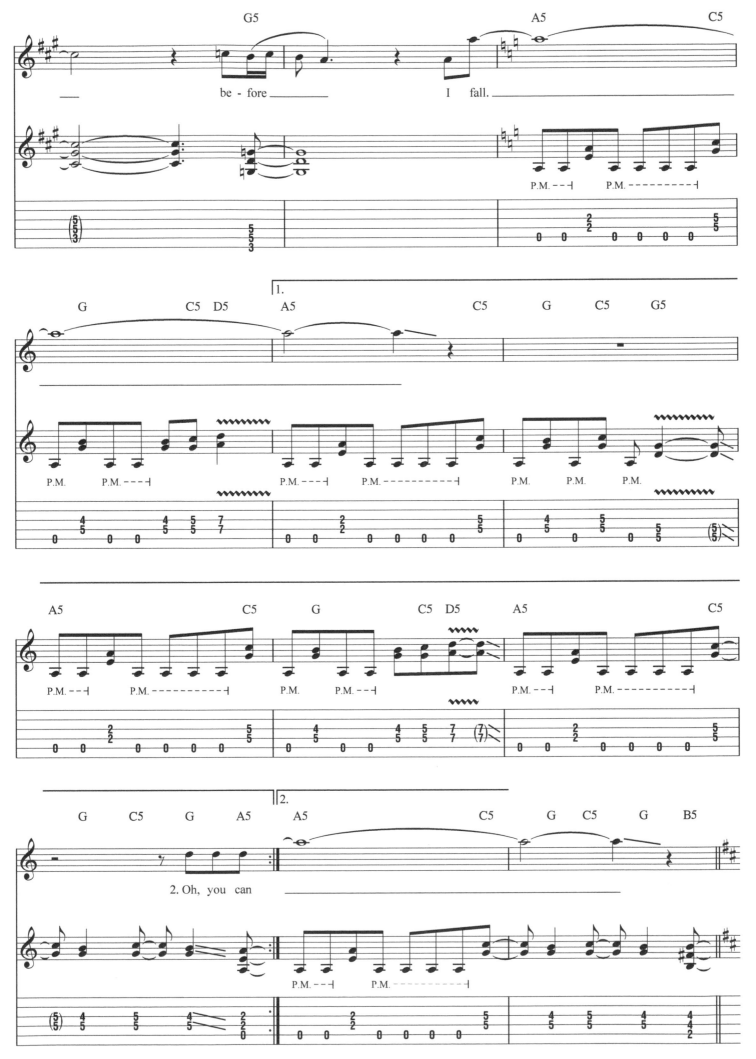

be - fore _____ I fall. _____

2. Oh, you can

On the high - way.

On the high - way.

Additional Lyrics

2. You can hang in a left or hang in a right;
   The choice it is yours to do as you might.
   The road is open wide to place your bidding.
   Now, wherever you turn, wherever you go,
   If you get it wrong, at least you can know
   There's miles and miles to put it back together.

3. Oh, making a curve or taking the strain,
   On the decline or out on the wane.
   Oh, ev'rybody breaks down sooner or later.
   We'll put it to rights, we'll square up and mend.
   Back on your feet to take the next bend.
   You'll weather ev'ry storm that's coming at ya.

Living After Midnight

Words and Music by Glenn Tipton, Rob Halford and K.K. Downing

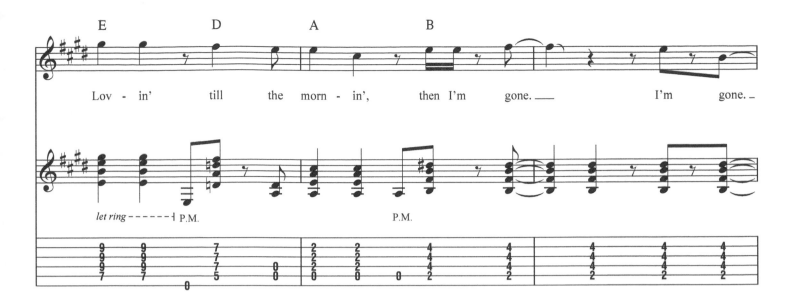

E   D   A   B

Lov - in' till the morn - in', then I'm gone. ___ I'm gone. ___

let ring ------ P.M.   P.M.

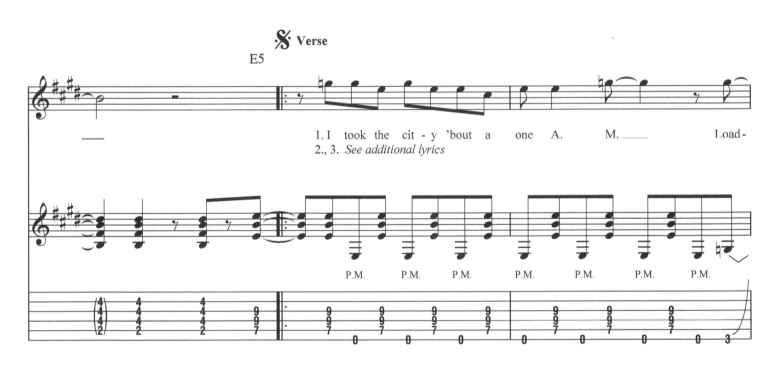

§ Verse

E5

1. I took the cit - y 'bout a one A. M. ___ Load-
2., 3. *See additional lyrics*

P.M.   P.M.   P.M.   P.M.   P.M.   P.M.   P.M.

- ed,   load - ed.   I'm all geared up to

1/4   P.M. ---------- ┤   1/4   P.M. -------- ┤ *let ring* ---------- ┤ P.M.   P.M.   P.M.

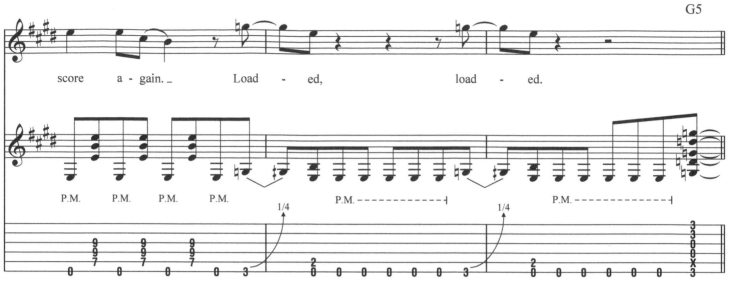

score a - gain. ___ Load - ed, load - ed.

Pre-Chorus

G5 F#5   B5

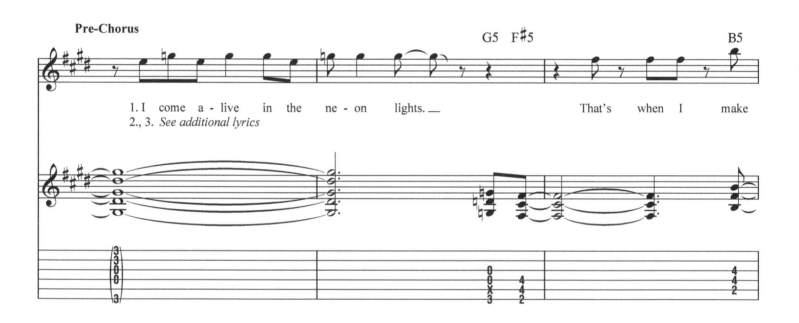

1. I come a - live in the ne - on lights. ___   That's when I make
2., 3. *See additional lyrics*

Chorus

To Coda ⊕

D5   E   D   A   B

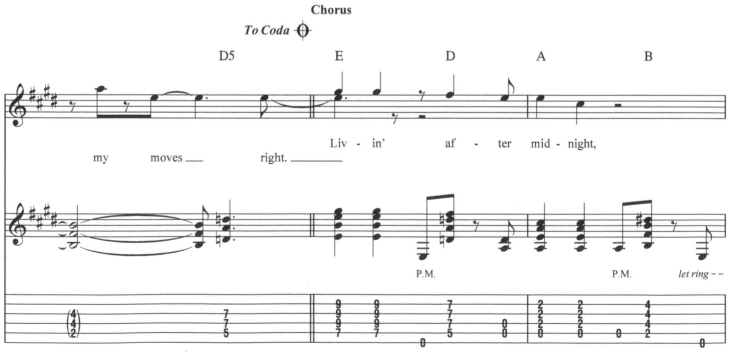

Liv - in' af - ter mid - night,

my moves ___ right. ___

rock - in'   to   the   dawn.   Lov - in'   till   the

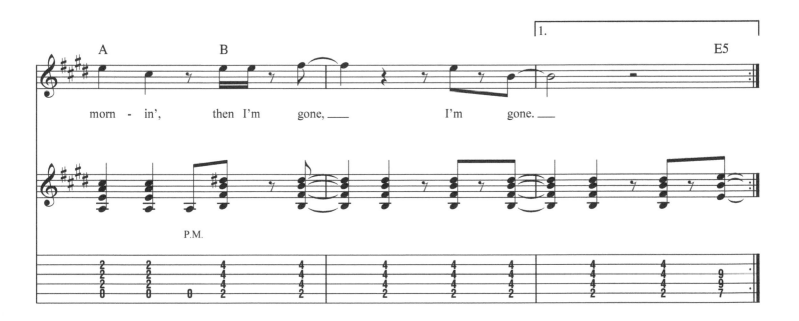

morn - in',   then   I'm   gone, ___   I'm   gone. ___

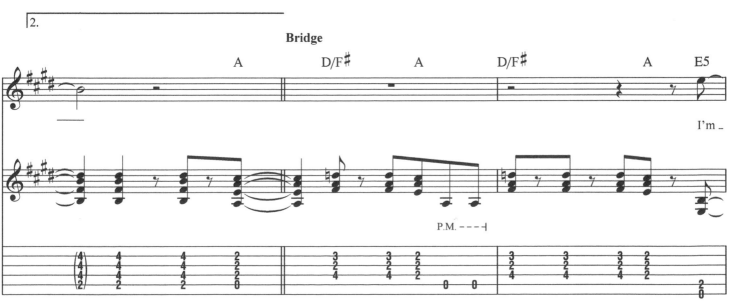

I'm _

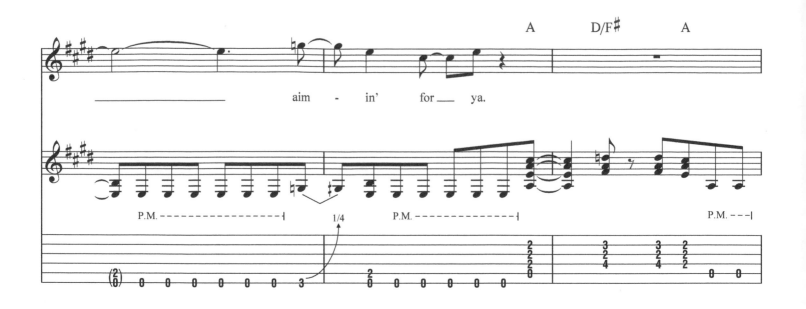

aim - in' for ___ ya.

I'm ___ gon - na floor ___ ya.

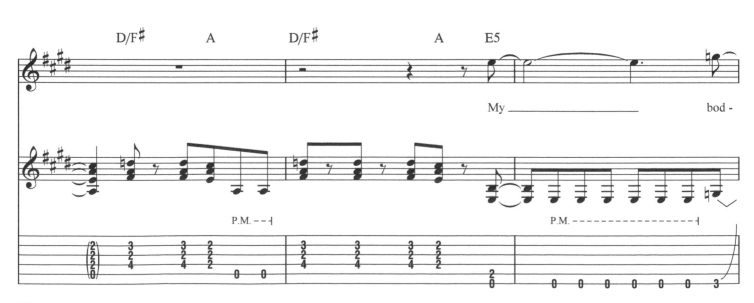

My ___ bod -

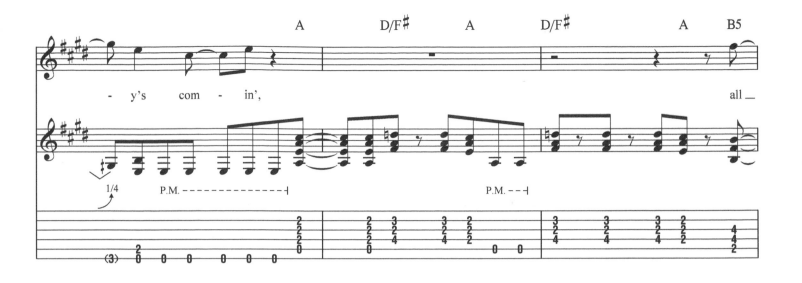

-y's com - in',   all __

Guitar Solo

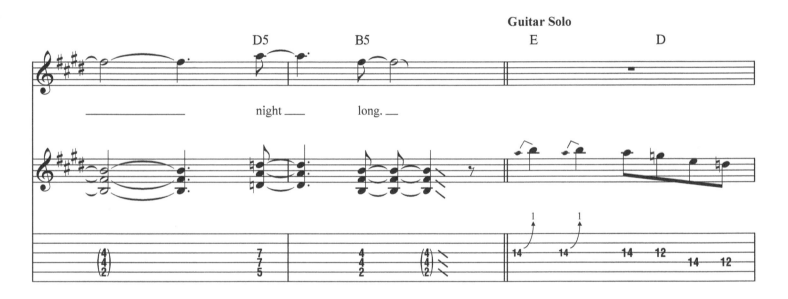

night __   long. __

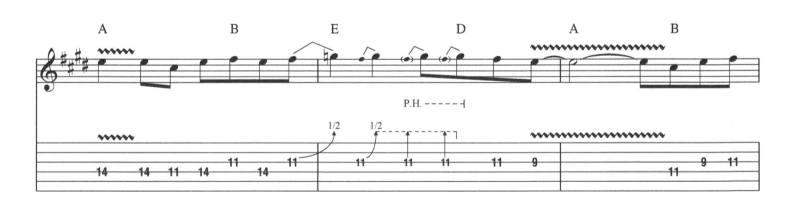

D.S. al Coda

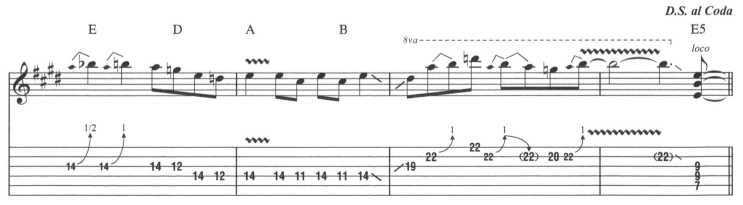

⊕ **Coda**
Outro-Chorus

Liv-in' af-ter mid-night, rock-in' to the dawn.

Repeat and fade

Lov-in' till the morn-in', then I'm gone, __ I'm gone. __

Additional Lyrics

2. Got gleamin' chrome reflecting feel.
Loaded, loaded.
Ready to take on ev'ry deal.
Loaded, loaded.

Pre-Chorus 2. My pulse is racin', hot to take.
But this motor's revved up, fit to break.

3. The air's electric, sparkin' power.
Loaded, loaded.
I'm gettin' harder by the hour.
Loaded, loaded.

Pre-Chorus 3. I set my sights and then home in.
The joints start fly'n' when I begin.

Painkiller

Words and Music by Glenn Raymond Tipton, Robert Halford and Kenneth Downing

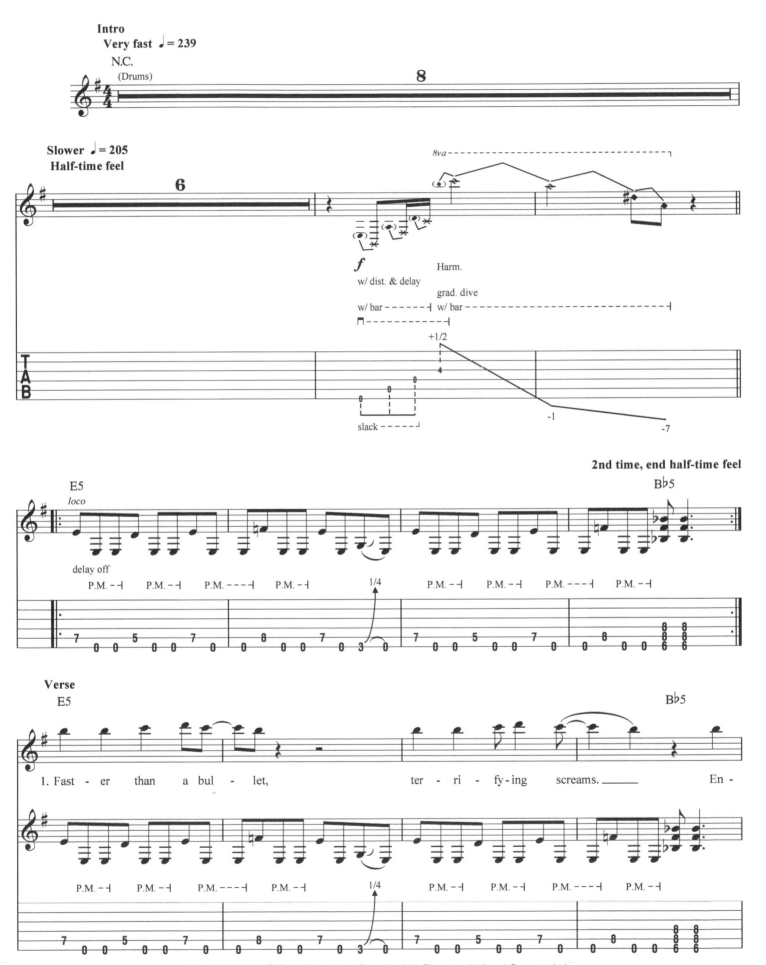

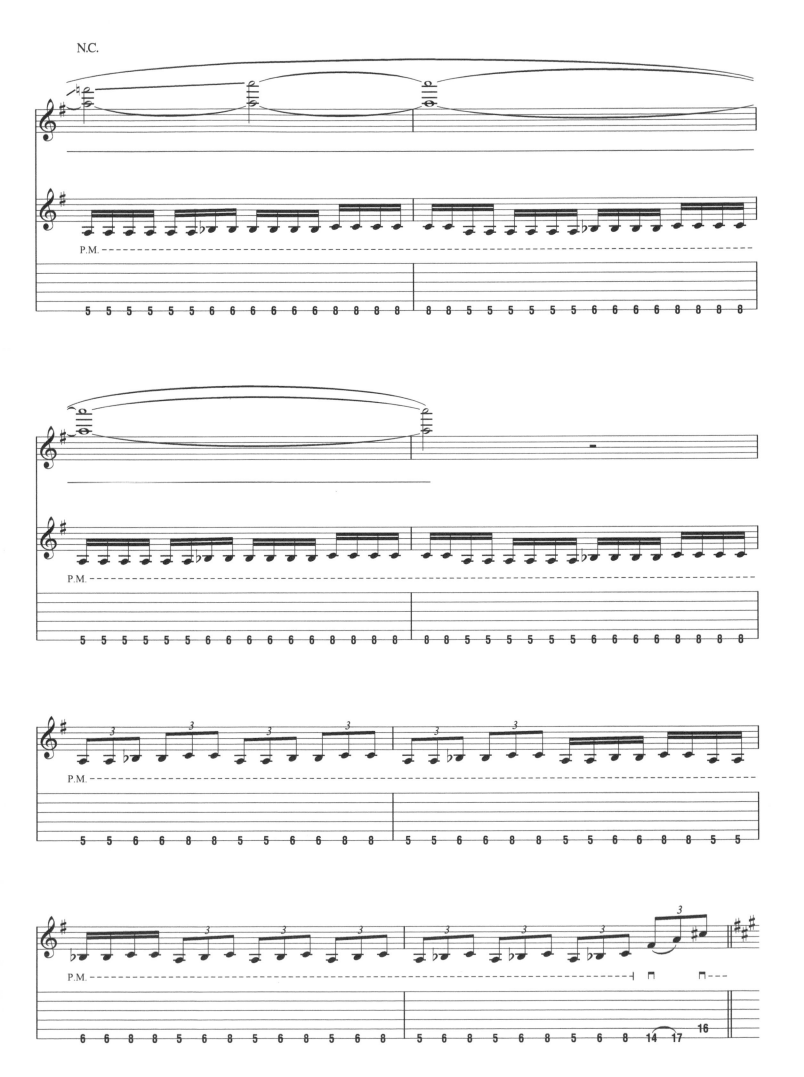

Guitar Solo

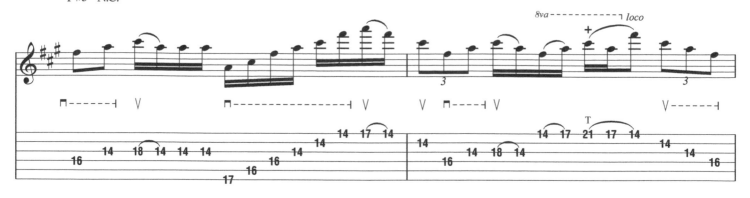

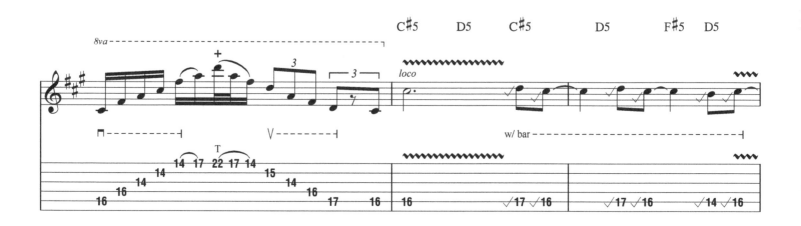

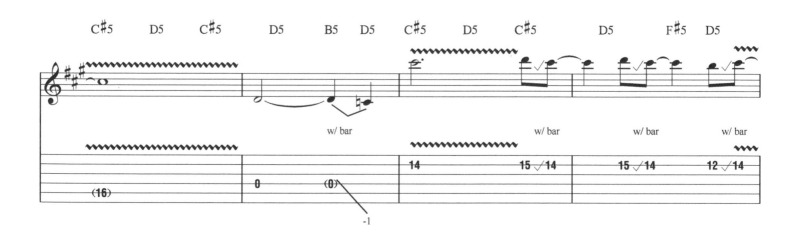

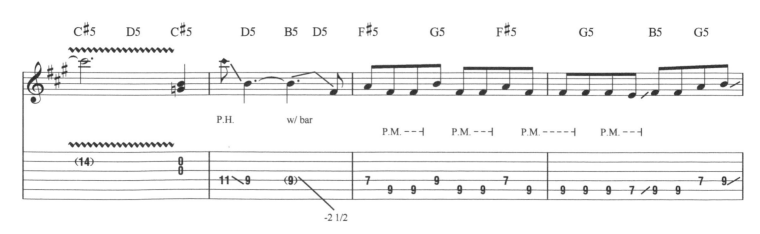

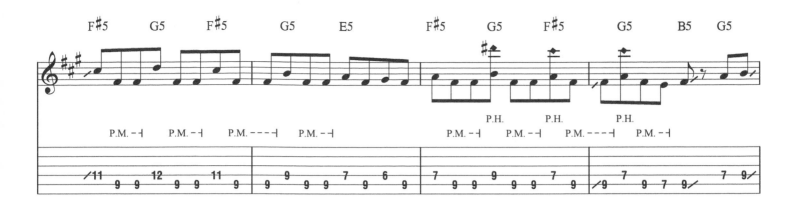

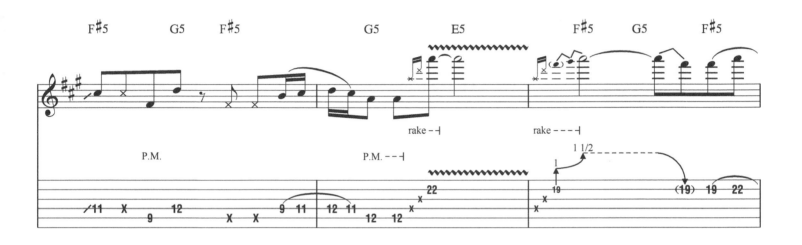

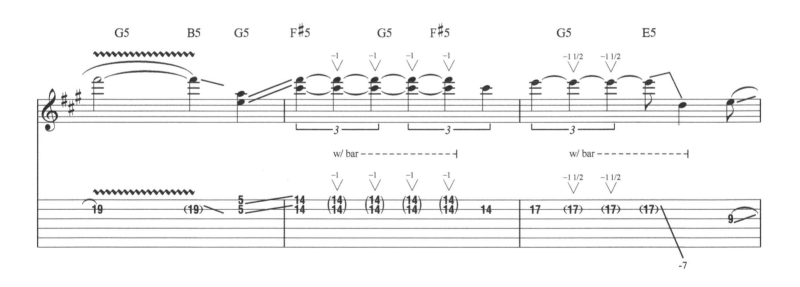

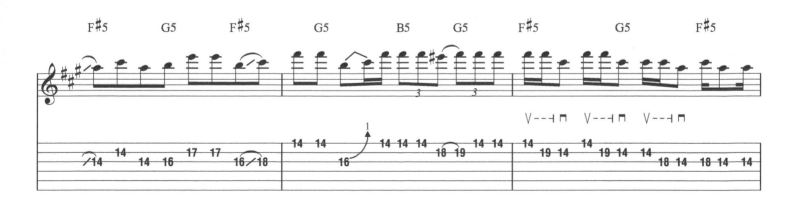

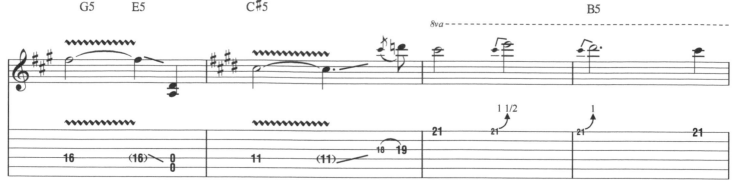

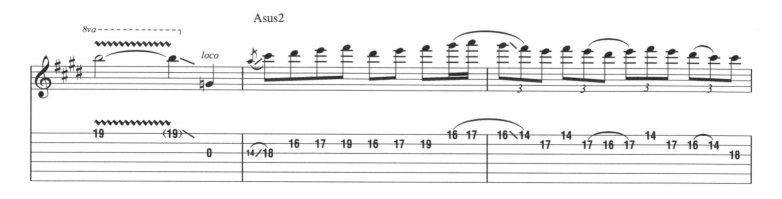

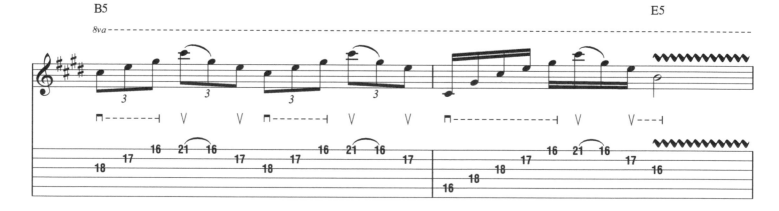

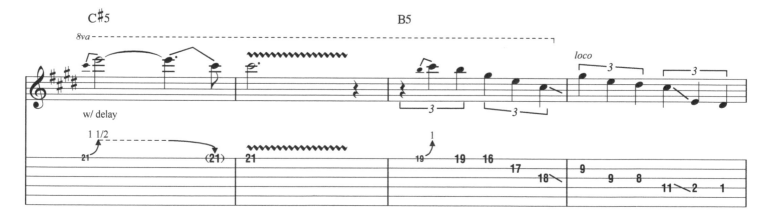

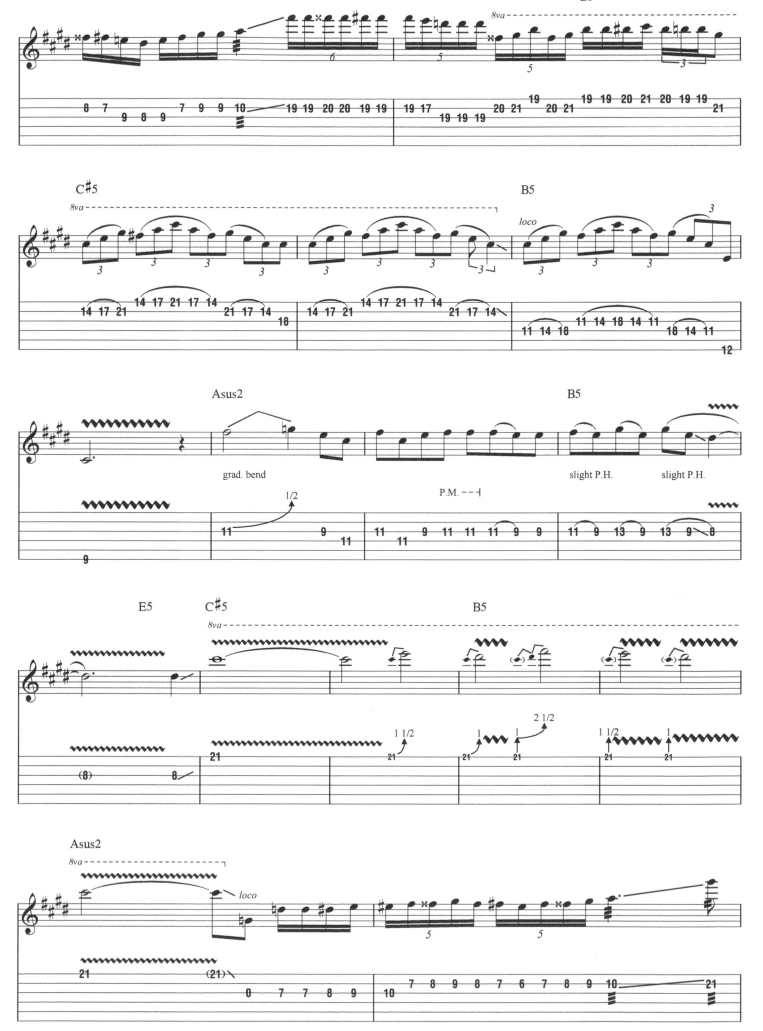

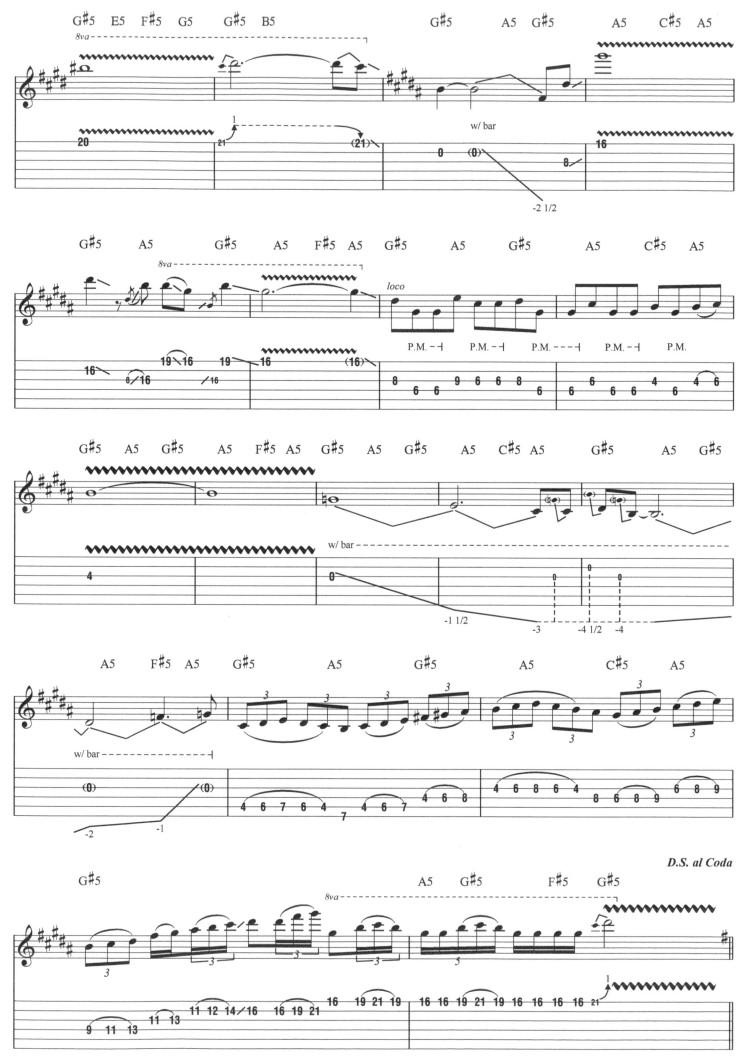

D.S. al Coda

Coda

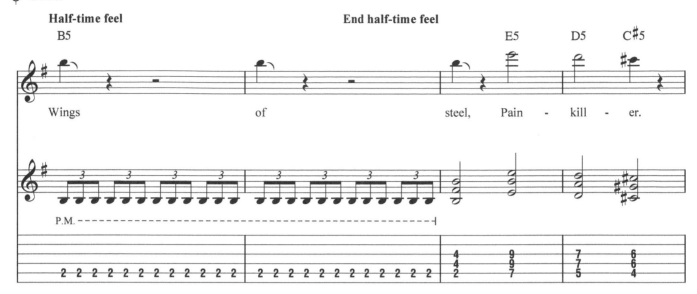

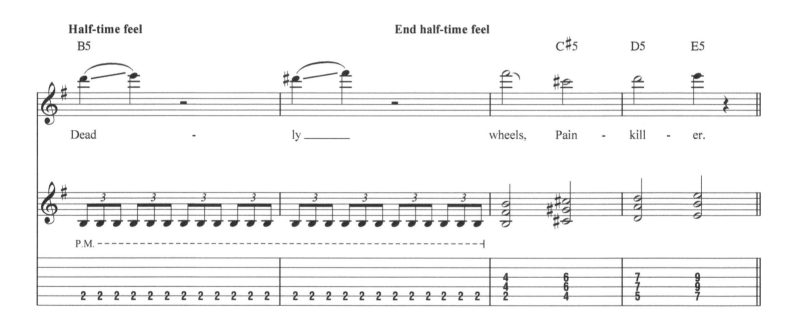

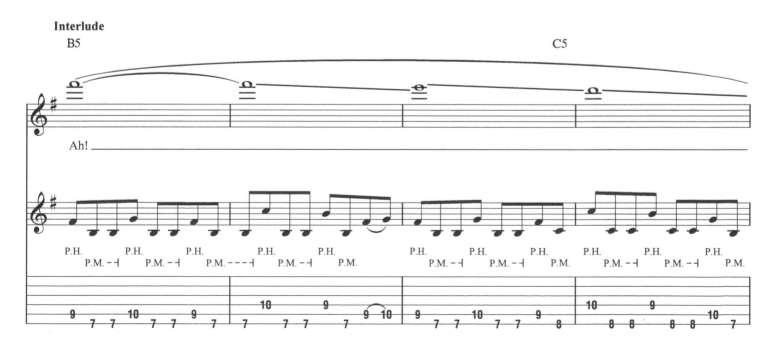

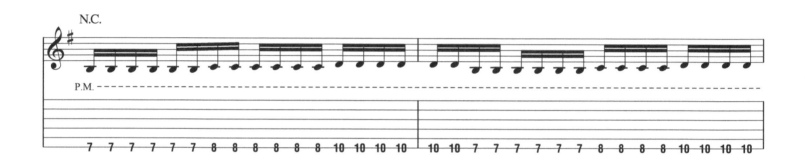

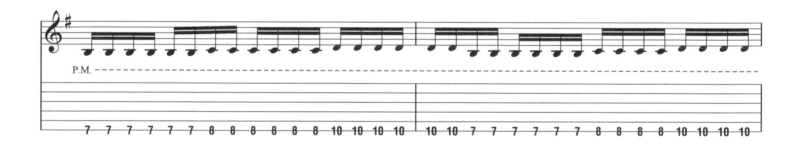

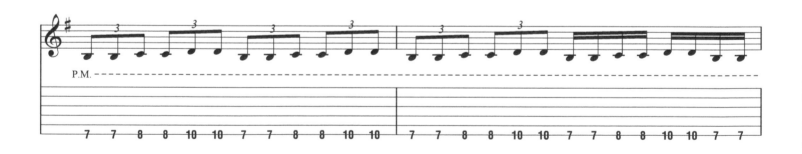

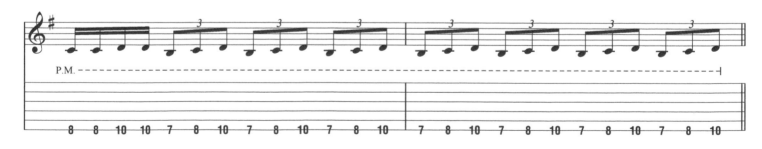

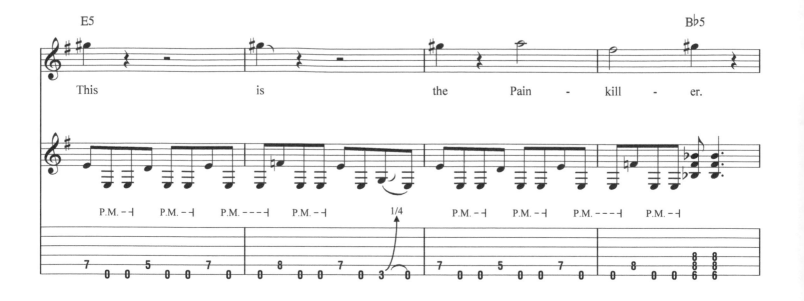

This   is   the Pain - kill - er.

Half-time feel

Pain,   Pain - kill - er,   kill - er.

End half-time feel

Pain,   Pain - kill - er,   kill - er._____

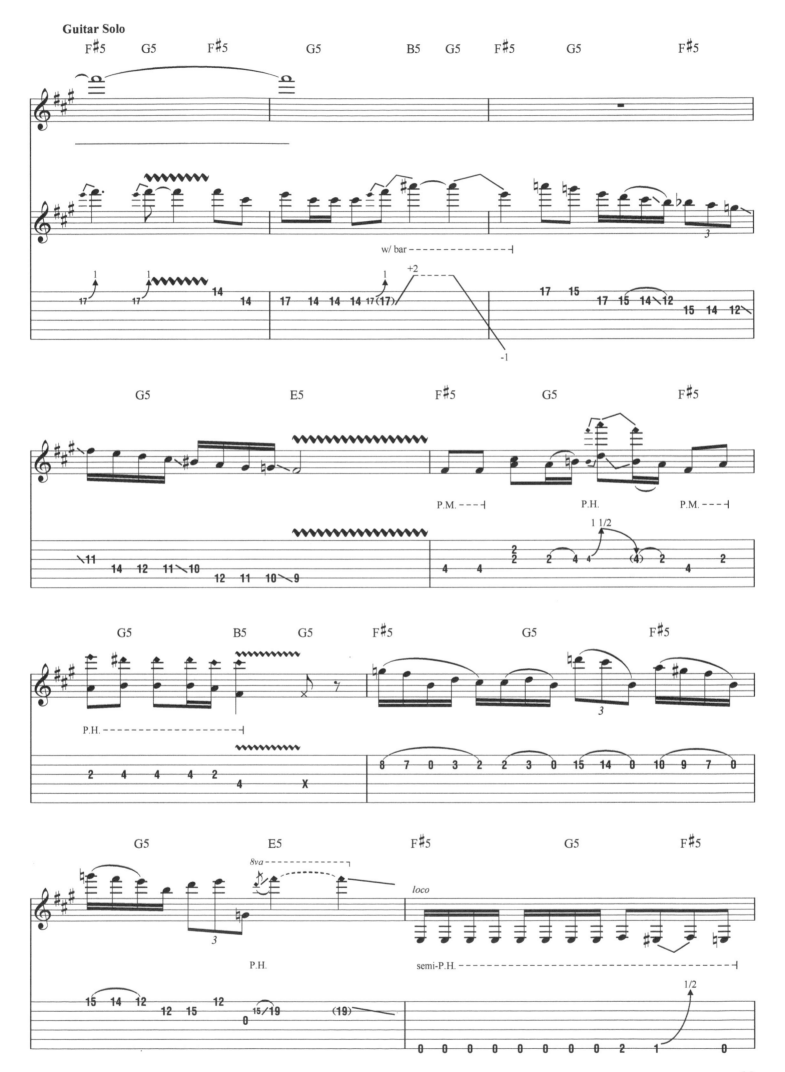

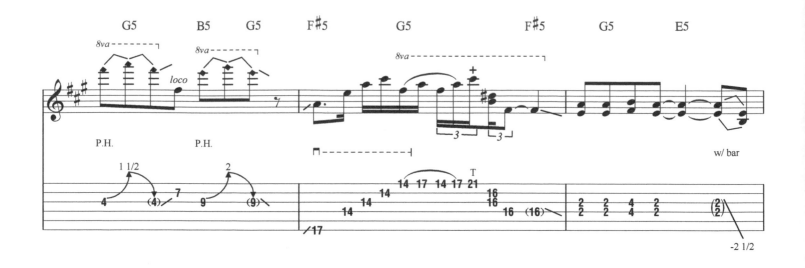

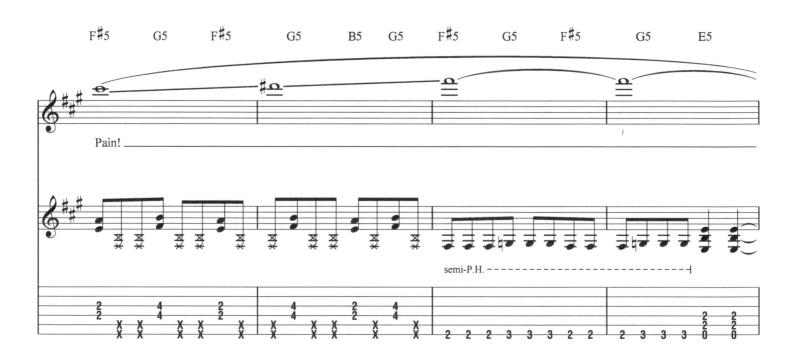

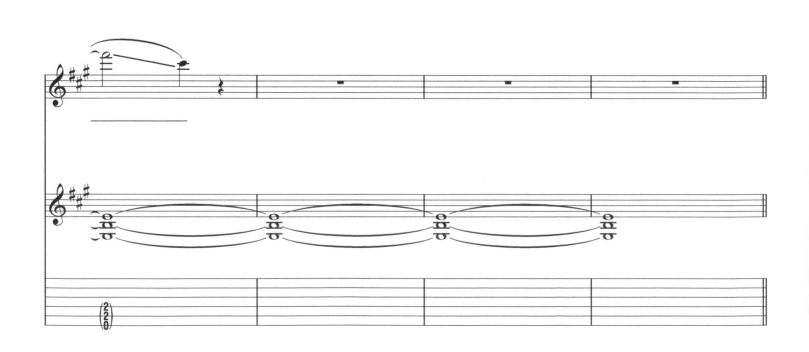

Outro

Free time

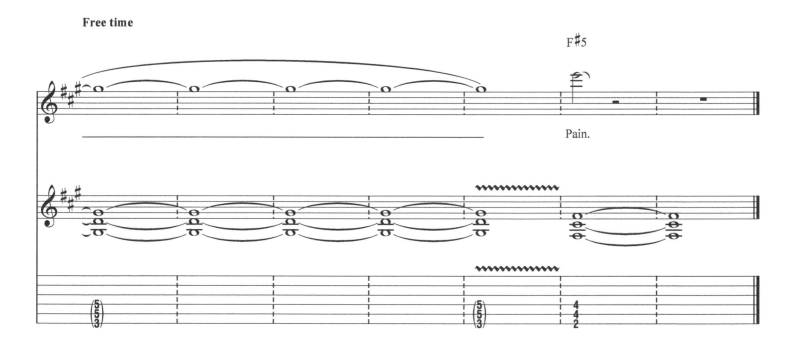

Additional Lyrics

3. Flying high on rapture, stronger, free and brave.
   Never more encaptured, they've been brought back from the grave.
   With mankind resurrected, forever to survive.
   Returns from Armageddon to the skies.

You've Got Another Thing Coming

Words and Music by Glenn Tipton, Rob Halford and K.K. Downing

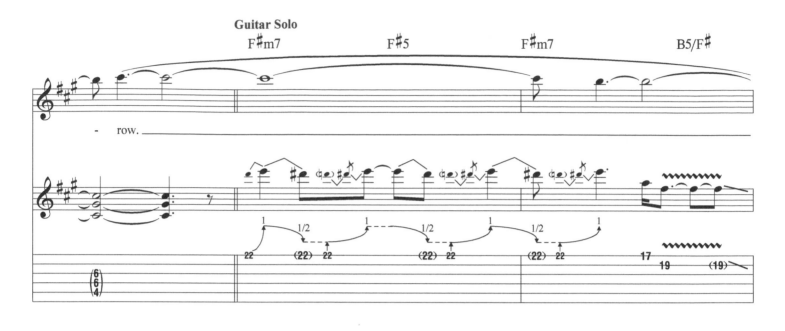

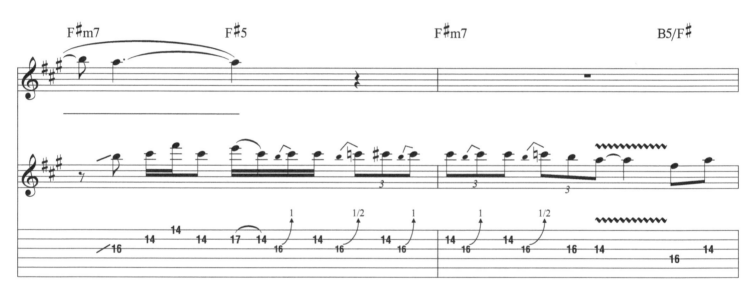

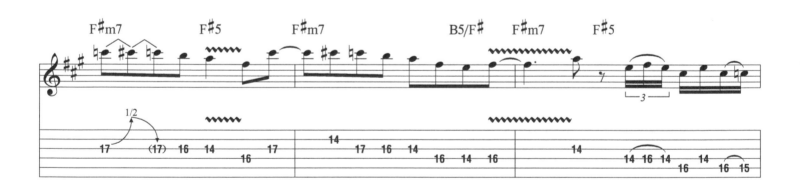

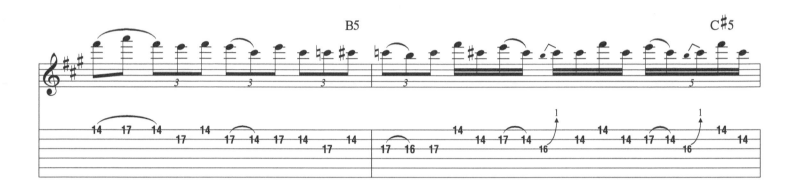

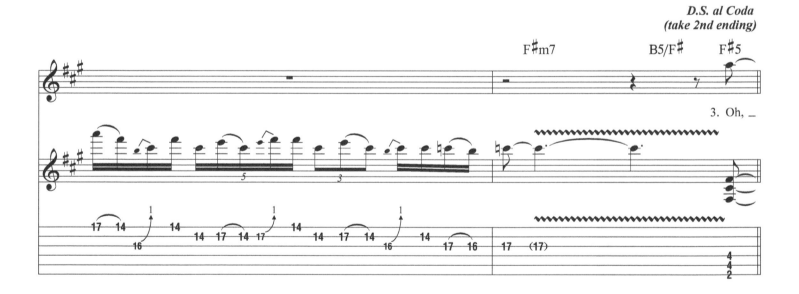

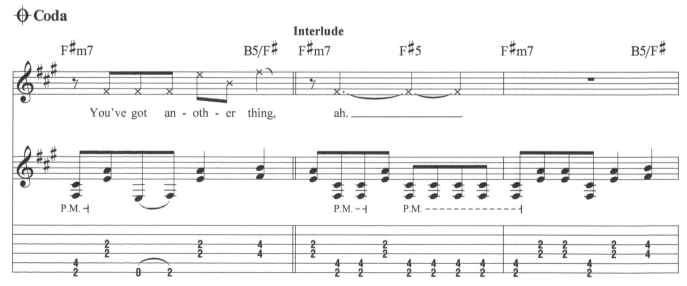

Com - in' on down!

Outro

Repeat and fade

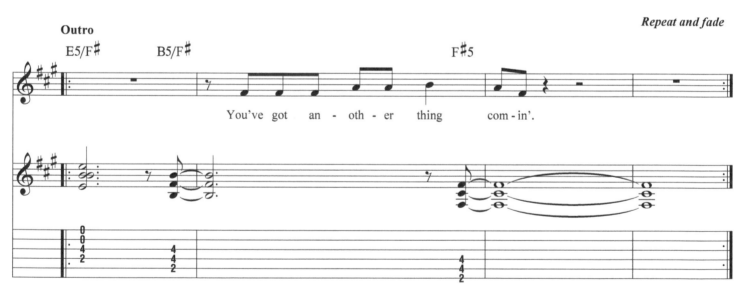

You've got an - oth - er thing com - in'.

Additional Lyrics

2. That's right, here's where the talking ends.
    Well listen, this night there'll be some action spent.
    Drive hard. Callin' all the shots.
    I got an ace card comin' down the rocks.

Pre-Chorus 2. If you think I'll sit around while you chip away my brain,
    Listen, I ain't foolin' and you'd better think again.
    Out there is a fortune waiting to be had.
    If you think I'll let it go you're mad.

3. Oh, so hot. No time to take a rest, yeah.
    Act tough, ain't room for second best.
    Real strong. Got me some security.
    Hey, I'm a big smash; I'm goin' for infinity, yeah.

HAL•LEONARD® GUITAR PLAY-ALONG

INCLUDES TAB

AUDIO ACCESS INCLUDED

This series will help you play your favorite songs quickly and easily. Just follow the tab and listen to the audio to hear how the guitar should sound, and then play along using the separate backing tracks.

Playback tools are provided for slowing down the tempo without changing pitch and looping challenging parts. The melody and lyrics are included in the book so that you can sing or simply follow along.

1. ROCK
00699570......$16.99

2. ACOUSTIC
00699569......$16.99

3. HARD ROCK
00699573......$17.99

4. POP/ROCK
00699571......$16.99

5. THREE CHORD SONGS
00300985......$16.99

6. '90S ROCK
00298615......$16.99

7. BLUES
00699575......$17.99

8. ROCK
00699585......$16.99

9. EASY ACOUSTIC SONGS
00151708......$16.99

10. ACOUSTIC
00699586......$16.95

11. EARLY ROCK
0699579......$15.99

12. ROCK POP
00291724......$16.99

14. BLUES ROCK
00699582......$16.99

15. R&B
00699583......$17.99

16. JAZZ
00699584......$16.99

17. COUNTRY
00699588......$16.99

18. ACOUSTIC ROCK
00699577......$15.95

20. ROCKABILLY
00699580......$16.99

21. SANTANA
00174525......$17.99

22. CHRISTMAS
00699600......$15.99

23. SURF
00699635......$16.99

24. ERIC CLAPTON
00699649......$17.99

25. THE BEATLES
00198265......$17.99

26. ELVIS PRESLEY
00699643......$16.99

27. DAVID LEE ROTH
00699645......$16.95

28. GREG KOCH
00699646......$17.99

29. BOB SEGER
00699647......$16.99

30. KISS
00699644......$16.99

32. THE OFFSPRING
00699653......$14.95

33. ACOUSTIC CLASSICS
00699656......$17.99

34. CLASSIC ROCK
00699658......$17.99

35. HAIR METAL
00699660......$17.99

36. SOUTHERN ROCK
00699661......$19.99

37. ACOUSTIC UNPLUGGED
00699662......$22.99

38. BLUES
00699663......$17.99

39. '80S METAL
00699664......$17.99

40. INCUBUS
00699668......$17.95

41. ERIC CLAPTON
00699669......$17.99

42. COVER BAND HITS
00211597......$16.99

43. LYNYRD SKYNYRD
00699681......$19.99

44. JAZZ GREATS
00699689......$16.99

45. TV THEMES
00699718......$14.95

46. MAINSTREAM ROCK
00699722......$16.95

47. HENDRIX SMASH HITS
00699723......$19.99

48. AEROSMITH CLASSICS
00699724......$17.99

49. STEVIE RAY VAUGHAN
00699725......$17.99

50. VAN HALEN 1978-1984
00110269......$19.99

51. ALTERNATIVE '90S
00699727......$14.99

52. FUNK
00699728......$15.99

53. DISCO
00699729......$14.99

54. HEAVY METAL
00699730......$17.99

55. POP METAL
00699731......$14.95

57. GUNS N' ROSES
00159922......$17.99

58. BLINK-182
00699772......$14.95

59. CHET ATKINS
00702347......$16.99

60. 3 DOORS DOWN
00699774......$14.95

62. CHRISTMAS CAROLS
00699798......$12.95

63. CREEDENCE CLEARWATER REVIVAL
00699802......$16.99

64. OZZY OSBOURNE
00699803......$17.99

66. THE ROLLING STONES
00699807......$17.99

67. BLACK SABBATH
00699808......$16.99

68. PINK FLOYD – DARK SIDE OF THE MOON
00699809......$17.99

71. CHRISTIAN ROCK
00699824......$14.95

72. ACOUSTIC '90S
00699827......$14.95

73. BLUESY ROCK
00699829......$16.99

74. SIMPLE STRUMMING SONGS
00151706......$19.99

75. TOM PETTY
00699882......$19.99

76. COUNTRY HITS
00699884......$16.99

77. BLUEGRASS
00699910......$17.99

78. NIRVANA
00700132......$16.99

79. NEIL YOUNG
00700133......$24.99

80. ACOUSTIC ANTHOLOGY
00700175......$19.95

81. ROCK ANTHOLOGY
00700176......$22.99

82. EASY ROCK SONGS
00700177......$17.99

84. STEELY DAN
00700200......$19.99

85. THE POLICE
00700269......$16.99

86. BOSTON
00700465......$16.99

87. ACOUSTIC WOMEN
00700763......$14.99

88. GRUNGE
00700467......$16.99

89. REGGAE
00700468......$15.99

90. CLASSICAL POP
00700469......$14.99

91. BLUES INSTRUMENTALS
00700505......$17.99

92. EARLY ROCK INSTRUMENTALS
00700506......$15.99

93. ROCK INSTRUMENTALS
00700507......$16.99

94. SLOW BLUES
00700508......$16.99

95. BLUES CLASSICS
00700509......$15.99

96. BEST COUNTRY HITS
00211615......$16.99

97. CHRISTMAS CLASSICS
00236542......$14.99

98. ROCK BAND
00700704......$14.95

99. ZZ TOP
00700762......$16.99

100. B.B. KING
00700466......$16.99

101. SONGS FOR BEGINNERS
00701917......$14.99

102. CLASSIC PUNK
00700769......$14.99

103. SWITCHFOOT
00700773......$16.99

104. DUANE ALLMAN
00700846......$17.99

105. LATIN
00700939 .... $16.99

106. WEEZER
00700958 .... $14.99

107. CREAM
00701069 .... $16.99

108. THE WHO
00701053 .... $16.99

109. STEVE MILLER
00701054 .... $19.99

110. SLIDE GUITAR HITS
00701055 .... $16.99

111. JOHN MELLENCAMP
00701056 .... $14.99

112. QUEEN
00701052 .... $16.99

113. JIM CROCE
00701058 .... $17.99

114. BON JOVI
00701060 .... $16.99

115. JOHNNY CASH
00701070 .... $16.99

116. THE VENTURES
00701124 .... $17.99

117. BRAD PAISLEY
00701224 .... $16.99

118. ERIC JOHNSON
00701353 .... $16.99

119. AC/DC CLASSICS
00701356 .... $17.99

120. PROGRESSIVE ROCK
00701457 .... $14.99

121. U2
00701508 .... $16.99

122. CROSBY, STILLS & NASH
00701610 .... $16.99

123. LENNON & McCARTNEY ACOUSTIC
00701614 .... $16.99

124. SMOOTH JAZZ
00200664 .... $16.99

125. JEFF BECK
00701687 .... $17.99

126. BOB MARLEY
00701701 .... $17.99

127. 1970S ROCK
00701739 .... $16.99

128. 1960S ROCK
00701740 .... $14.99

129. MEGADETH
00701741 .... $17.99

130. IRON MAIDEN
00701742 .... $17.99

131. 1990S ROCK
00701743 .... $14.99

132. COUNTRY ROCK
00701757 .... $15.99

133. TAYLOR SWIFT
00701894 .... $16.99

134. AVENGED SEVENFOLD
00701906 .... $16.99

135. MINOR BLUES
00151350 .... $17.99

136. GUITAR THEMES
00701922 .... $14.99

137. IRISH TUNES
00701966 .... $15.99

138. BLUEGRASS CLASSICS
00701967 .... $17.99

139. GARY MOORE
00702370 .... $16.99

140. MORE STEVIE RAY VAUGHAN
00702396 .... $17.99

141. ACOUSTIC HITS
00702401 .... $16.99

142. GEORGE HARRISON
00237697 .... $17.99

143. SLASH
00702425 .... $19.99

144. DJANGO REINHARDT
00702531 .... $16.99

145. DEF LEPPARD
00702532 .... $19.99

146. ROBERT JOHNSON
00702533 .... $16.99

147. SIMON & GARFUNKEL
14041591 .... $16.99

148. BOB DYLAN
14041592 .... $16.99

149. AC/DC HITS
14041593 .... $17.99

150. ZAKK WYLDE
02501717 .... $19.99

151. J.S. BACH
02501730 .... $16.99

152. JOE BONAMASSA
02501751 .... $19.99

153. RED HOT CHILI PEPPERS
00702990 .... $19.99

155. ERIC CLAPTON – FROM THE ALBUM UNPLUGGED
00703085 .... $16.99

156. SLAYER
00703770 .... $19.99

157. FLEETWOOD MAC
00101382 .... $17.99

159. WES MONTGOMERY
00102593 .... $19.99

160. T-BONE WALKER
00102641 .... $17.99

161. THE EAGLES – ACOUSTIC
00102659 .... $17.99

162. THE EAGLES HITS
00102667 .... $17.99

163. PANTERA
00103036 .... $17.99

164. VAN HALEN 1986-1995
00110270 .... $17.99

165. GREEN DAY
00210343 .... $17.99

166. MODERN BLUES
00700764 .... $16.99

167. DREAM THEATER
00111938 .... $24.99

168. KISS
00113421 .... $17.99

169. TAYLOR SWIFT
00115982 .... $16.99

170. THREE DAYS GRACE
00117337 .... $16.99

171. JAMES BROWN
00117420 .... $16.99

172. THE DOOBIE BROTHERS
00116970 .... $16.99

173. TRANS-SIBERIAN ORCHESTRA
00119907 .... $19.99

174. SCORPIONS
00122119 .... $16.99

175. MICHAEL SCHENKER
00122127 .... $17.99

176. BLUES BREAKERS WITH JOHN MAYALL & ERIC CLAPTON
00122132 .... $19.99

177. ALBERT KING
00123271 .... $16.99

178. JASON MRAZ
00124165 .... $17.99

179. RAMONES
00127073 .... $16.99

180. BRUNO MARS
00129706 .... $16.99

181. JACK JOHNSON
00129854 .... $16.99

182. SOUNDGARDEN
00138161 .... $17.99

183. BUDDY GUY
00138240 .... $17.99

184. KENNY WAYNE SHEPHERD
00138258 .... $17.99

185. JOE SATRIANI
00139457 .... $17.99

186. GRATEFUL DEAD
00139459 .... $17.99

187. JOHN DENVER
00140839 .... $17.99

188. MÖTLEY CRUE
00141145 .... $17.99

189. JOHN MAYER
00144350 .... $17.99

190. DEEP PURPLE
00146152 .... $17.99

191. PINK FLOYD CLASSICS
00146164 .... $17.99

192. JUDAS PRIEST
00151352 .... $17.99

193. STEVE VAI
00156028 .... $19.99

194. PEARL JAM
00157925 .... $17.99

195. METALLICA: 1983-1988
00234291 .... $19.99

196. METALLICA: 1991-2016
00234292 .... $19.99